LOST TRAMWAYS OF ENGLAND
LONDON SOUTH-EAST

PETER WALLER

GRAFFEG

CONTENTS

LONDON SOUTH-EAST

1. Elephant & Castle
2. Dog Kennel Hill
3. Westhorne Avenue
4. Brockley
5. East Wickham
6. Plumpstead

7. Woolwich
8. Borough
9. Bermondsey
10. Bricklayers Arms
11. Camberwell Green

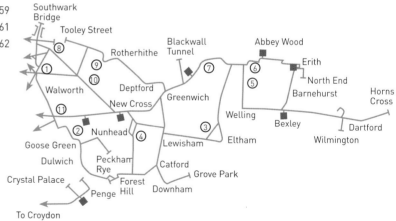

INTRODUCTION

Although there had been street tramways in Britain from the early 1860s in places like Birkenhead and London, it was not until the 1870 Tramways Act that a legislative framework was established for their construction and operation. The Act empowered local authorities to grant licences to companies to operate tramways for a 21-year period. The licensee could construct the tramway itself or the route could be constructed by the local authority and leased as part of the franchise to the operator. Initially, it was expected that private companies would always operate the tramways built; however, in 1883, Huddersfield Corporation in the West Riding of Yorkshire, having constructed a new steam tramway to serve the town, was unable to find a licensee willing to take on operation and so became the first municipal operator of trams within the British Isles.

The 1870 Act imposed a number of restrictions upon the tramway builder and operator; with the benefit of hindsight, it can be seen that these had a negative impact upon tramway development in the United Kingdom and undoubtedly represented one factor in the demise of the tramcar from the 1920s onwards. One of these clauses required the builder and operator of the tramway to maintain the public highway to a distance of 18 inches outside each running line; this effectively made the tramway owner responsible for the upkeep of the road surface on those streets where trams operated. At a time when the condition of the public highway was often poor, the well-built and well-maintained section over which the trams operated became a magnet for other road users. As road traffic increased, so trams – despite the fact that the road had been constructed to accommodate them – were increasingly perceived as a cause of road traffic delays.

The second weakness within the 1870 Act was the so-called 'scrap iron clause'; this permitted the licensor – usually the local authority – to take over the assets (such as the trams) owned by the licensee at asset value – including depreciation – rather than reflecting the value of the business. As a result, tramway licensees became increasingly unwilling to invest in their business as the licence period came towards its end. The Act permitted the termination of the licence after 21 years and every seven years thereafter. For company-owned operations this sword of Damocles meant that the threat of municipalisation was ever present and, even if never exercised, was sufficient to ensure that modernisation might never take place. The classic example here is the tramways of Bristol; operated throughout their career by a company but with the constant threat of takeover by Bristol Corporation, the system survived through until 1941 operating open-top and unvestibuled trams that would not have been out of place on the first electric tramways built at the end of the 19th century whereas other systems were operating state-of-the-art modern trams by World War II.

This volume is one of a series that cover the tramways of England and is one of four looking at the tramways of London. This volume examines the history of the tramways that operated on the south-east side of the Thames.

Bexley UDC tramways

Although there were earlier proposals for the construction of a network of 3ft 6in gauge tramways within the UDC when Royal Assent was granted on 26 July 1901 to the Bexley Tramways Act 1901, the use of standard gauge had been decided. The Act empowered the UDC to construct just over 5¼ route miles from Plumstead via Welling and Bexley to Gravel Hill and a branch from Bexley via Bexleyheath to Northumberland Heath, where a connection was made with the tramways operated by Erith UDC following the opening of the latter's tramways on 26 August 1905.

The official opening of the Bexley tramway took place on 3 October 1903. For the opening of the system, 12 open-top double-deck trams were supplied by the Preston-based Electric Railway & Tramway Carriage Works Ltd. These were originally fitted with Brush Type A four-wheel trucks, but these were later replaced by Peckham P22 four-wheel trucks. In order to supplement the existing fleet, a further four identical trams were acquired in 1904.

In order to facilitate the construction of the London County Council LCC standard-gauge route to Abbey Wood, which replaced the 3ft 6in horse tramway of the Woolwich & South East London Co, a short section of track in Plumstead High Street was transferred to the LCC on 21 July 1908; in exchange for this, Bexley UDC was granted rights to operate from Plumstead to Woolwich over LCC track and a through service from Woolwich to Bexleyheath was introduced on 26 July 1908.

The outbreak of war in August 1914 brought additional traffic to the tramways and a number of trams were hired from the LCC; the operation of these required the modification to the overhead as it passed under the railway bridge at Welling due to the extra height of the hired trams and 12 ex-LCC trams were in service by 1917, including six that had been purchased.

In August 1917, fire destroyed the tramcar fleet operated by the Dartford Council Light Railways, with Bexley UDC stepping into the breach to operate a skeleton service on its neighbour's route; thereafter, until the creation of the London Passenger Transport Board (LPTB), the tramways of Bexley and Dartford were managed by a joint committee from – effectively – 1 April 1921.

Dartford Council Light Railways

The tramways within Dartford were authorised under the terms of the Light Railways Act of 1896, with the relevant Order being confirmed on 6 February 1902. Additional powers were obtained later the same year and in 1903 before work on construction commenced. In all, about 6½ route miles were constructed. The network stretched from Gravel Hill, where a connection was eventually made with the Bexley UDC system during World War I, via Crayford and Dartford to Horns Cross, with two short branches in the town centre, north to Victoria Road and south to Wilmington.

To operate the new tramway, 12 open-top double-deck trams, fitted with Brill 21E four-wheel trucks, were acquired from the United Electric Car Co Ltd. These were delivered in time for the opening of the system on 14 February 1906. Operation of the system was leased to Balfour Beatty in 1909.

Traffic on the Dartford system again grew significantly as a result of the war effort and, in order to supplement its fleet, one of the redundant demi cars operated by Erith UDC was purchased in 1916. This became No 13 in the Dartford fleet and was utilised on the Wilmington route. It was not to survive long with its new owner, however, as, overnight on 6/7 August 1917, the entire Dartford fleet was destroyed by a fire in the depot. Investigation of the incident suggested that it had been started by a carelessly disposed of cigarette stub. The fire also completely destroyed the depot. Fortunately, Bexley UDC was able to provide a much-reduced service initially and then hired an additional 12 trams from the LCC to ensure that a full service was restored. It was agreed *pro tem* that Bexley UDC would operate the service and be reimbursed for the cost of the vehicles pending the reconstruction of the depot and the purchase of new trams. In the event this was not to take place and the tramways were subsequently operated by Bexley under the aegis of a joint committee.

Erith UDC tramways

On 14 August 1903 the Erith Tramways and Improvements Act 1903 received the Royal Assent. The Act permitted the Urban District Council to construct a number of routes within its area. Work on the construction commenced during 1904 and, on 26 August 1905, the new electric tramcar services were officially inaugurated; of the almost six route miles authorised by the original Act, a total of 4¾ route miles had been completed. This comprised a main route from Abbey Wood – close to the future terminus of the London County Council route to Abbey Wood (there was to be no physical connection between the two systems until after the creation of the London Passenger Transport Board in 1933) – to Erith town centre, where the line divided, with one branch heading along Bexley Road to an end-on connection with the tramways of Bexley at Northumberland Heath and another to North End via Crayford Road. The physical connection with the Bexley system eventually permitted a through service between the two towns to operate until this was withdrawn on 25 July 1914 following a dispute about the sharing of revenue; it was subsequently to be reinstated.

For the opening of the system, a total of 14 double-deck trams were ordered from the Loughborough-based Brush. Of these, Nos 1-6 and 9 were open-top whilst Nos 7, 8 and 10-14 had open-balcony top covers. All were fitted with Mountain & Gibson 21EM four-wheel trucks. These were originally of 6ft 0in wheelbase but were replaced with 8ft 0in wheelbase trucks after World War I. In 1906 a further two trams – Nos 15 and 16 – were acquired from G. C. Milnes, Voss & Co Ltd. These were single-deck demi cars that were fitted with Mountain & Gibson special four-wheel trucks of 5ft 6in wheelbase. Smaller than conventional trams, each of these could accommodate 20 seated passengers. The two were designed for use on the North End service where the route was losing money.

The use of the demi cars on the North End service did little to improve the service's finances and between January 1909 and 11 June 1910 the service was suspended. Briefly in operation again, the service from the town centre to North End was abandoned on 31 August 1910. This left the sole service as Abbey Wood to Northumberland Heath.

During World War I the two demi cars were sold – No 15 to Dartford and No 16 to Doncaster – with four second-hand trams being acquired from London United Tramways and a fifth from Hull Corporation to in order to cater for the additional traffic that arose as a result of the conflict, having previously hired a number of trams to assist with the war effort.

After the war the Erith tramways continued to struggle financially, although both the track and overhead were renewed post-war and the ex-LUT cars rebuilt. Encompassing just over four route miles with a fleet of 19 passenger trams and one works car, Erith UDC represented the smallest tramway operator to be incorporated into the LPTB on 1 July 1933.

Joyce Green Hospital Tramways

Not all of the tramways within south-east London were destined to become part of the LPTB. In the early 1890s it was decided to construct a hospital complex on Dartford marshes to cater for patients suffering from smallpox and other illnesses requiring isolation. In order to serve the site, a network of 4ft 0in gauge tramways was constructed between 1897 and 1902. The system was provided with a number of horse-drawn tramcars, although, from 1925, these were hauled by motor ambulances (the idea of acquiring Simplex petrol-operated railway engines having been discounted due to the need to relay the track to accommodate the additional weight). The hospital complex passed to the LCC in 1930 but operation of the tramway ceased in 1936.

Bexley UDC Tramways & Dartford Light Railways Joint Committee

Following the August 1917 fire, Bexley UDC hired – and subsequently purchased – a number of ex-LCC 'B' class trams; in all, 23 were operated (six hired and returned along with 17 purchased).

Balfour Beatty's lease expired on 31 March 1921 and agreement was made between Bexley and Dartford councils for a joint committee to operate the trams. The agreement, backdated to 1 April 1921, was signed on 6 February 1922. This was to manage the tramway through until it was subsumed into the LPTB on 1 July 1933.

London County Council routes

The LCC network developed from a number of earlier horse tramways in the area; some of these were existing LCC routes but others were acquired from companies as and when leases expired. Although the majority of these were standard gauge, there was one – the Woolwich & South East London Tramways Co – that had adopted the 3ft 6in gauge; this required rebuilding to standard gauge before electric trams could commence operation. The work involved in electrification was substantially more complicated than for most tramways, given that the LCC decided to adopt the conduit system of power supply for the bulk of its network; this necessitated much more substantial excavation and was also more costly.

The first LCC electric trams to operate over the sections featured in this volume were two routes from Blackfriars and Southwark bridges to Greenwich; that via Elephant & Castle, Old Kent Road and New Cross Road opened on 17 January 1904 whilst that via Camberwell, Peckham and New Cross followed exactly a week later.

The section from New Cross to Lewisham opened on 30 January 1906. The route from Greenwich to Blackwall Tunnel opened in two stages from Greenwich to Blackwall Lane on 10 June 1906 and then to the tunnel eight days later. Greenwich to Lewisham via South Street opened on 4 April 1908. The route was extended through to Charlton – where the new Central Repair Depot was established – on 22 March 1909; it was extended through to Woolwich in two stages, opening on 1 April 1911 and 5 April 1914.

Camberwell to Dulwich also opened in two stages: from Camberwell to Crystal Palace Road on 19 November 1906 and thence to Dulwich on 20 December 1906. The section included the steep Dog Kennel Hill; restrictions on the number of trams that could be on the gradient at the same time led to this part of the route being quadrupled, with the additional tracks being brought into use on 6 April 1912.

The route from Lewisham to Eltham Church was opened in three stages: initially to Lea Green on 4 May 1907, then to Lyme Farm on 29 November 1920 and finally to Eltham Church of 22 March 1921.

The branch to Peckham Rye opened on 28 November 1907, with the extension from Dulwich to Forest Hill following on 19 December 1908. The route from Woolwich via Plumstead to Abbey Wood opened on 26 July 1908; this included a short section taken over from Bexley UDC and resulted in Bexley cars running through to Woolwich; this was the first occasion on which the LCC introduced a joint service. The section from Woolwich Ferry to Abbey Wood was the LCC's first section equipped with overhead and resulted in the first change pit – a feature of the London system through to final closure – being installed.

The opening from the line from Woolwich to Eltham on 23 July 1909 was complicated by the proximity of the tram route to Greenwich Observatory; this resulted in the overhead initially being dual wired – both positive and negative – rather than the more usual negative return via the track in order to avoid possible interference with the equipment.

The route from the Red Lion at Dockhead to Bermondsey Street opened on 25 February 1911; it was extended from the Red Lion to Deptford Creek Bridge on 22 June 1911 and thence into

Greenwich on 5 August 1911. The section from Bermondsey Street to Stanier Street opened on 28 November 1911 and thence to the final terminus adjacent to London Bridge station on 9 December 1912.

The section from Lewisham to Forest Hill opened in three stages – on 26 February 1910 (to Brockley Lane station), on 25 February 1911 (to Crofton Park) and finally to Forest Hill on 13 August 1915. The route from Lewisham to Catford opened on 29 May 1913.

The Grove Park section from Catford – designed to serve eventually a new housing estate – opened to Bellingham on 5 April 1914 and thence to Southend on 9 April 1914; the route finally reached Grove Park on 15 November 1928, having previously opened from Southend to Valeswood Road on 28 September 1926 and thence to Southover on 28 July 1927.

The final LCC extension – along Westhorne Avenue – opened on 30 June 1932; this was part of a plan to extend through to Grove Park; work on this extension had not commenced by the time the LPTB took over and it was never completed.

The LPTB takes over

On 1 July 1933, the existing operators in south-east London came under common ownership and operation for the first time.

The single biggest operator was the LCC; a total of almost 158 route miles and 1,663 trams were operated throughout the Metropolis by the LCC, including most of those that served the area of London covered by this volume.

The combined Bexley UDC & Dartford Light Railways operated a fleet of 33 trams over a network of just over 11½ route miles. The fleet numbers 2066-98 were allocated by the LPTB to the 33 but the trams were never renumbered and the numbers were subsequently reallocated to ex-MET 'Felthams'. Bexley Nos 1-16 were withdrawn almost immediately after the creation of the LPTB, being replaced by ex-LCC trams, whilst Nos 17-33, which were second-hand ex-LCC 'B' class, were given some attention and received a 'C' suffix after their original Bexley number. However, all had been withdrawn by the end of 1933 and replaced by further ex-LCC cars.

The network inherited from Erith UDC represented, at just over four route miles, the smallest of the pre-LPTB tramways taken over in 1933. In addition, Erith also operated, under lease from Bexley, the 1¼-mile section from Bexleyheath to Northumberland Heath. The 19 ex-Erith trams were – Nos 1-19 – were given the 'D' suffix and allocated the fleet numbers – never carried – of 2099-117. All of the ex-Erith trams had been withdrawn and scrapped by the end of 1935.

Although the LCC had no plans for tramcar replacement – indeed, it had invested a significant amount in new trams in the years prior to the creation of the LPTB – the LPTB was keen on conversion to trolleybus operation and in 1934 powers were obtained for the first phase of the conversion programme. Amongst the routes affected were those in Bexley and Erith.

Before this work commenced, a short section of line opened in Abbey Wood on 18 December 1933 to connect the lines taken over from Erith and the LCC; this permitted the closure of Erith depot, as the required trams were thereafter based at the LCC's depot at Abbey Wood.

The trolleybuses arrive

The first conversion in the south-east after the LPTB takeover was on 19 April 1934, when the short Wilmington route in Dartford was replaced by a Country Area bus service. In October 1934 the services between Horns Cross and Woolwich and between Abbey Wood and Bexleyheath were allocated the fleet numbers 96 and 98 respectively.

Trams were not to carry these route numbers for long. On 10 November 1935 the 98 was converted to trolleybus operation – as route 698 – and extended westwards to serve Woolwich. A fortnight later, on the 24th, it was the turn of the 96 which became trolleybus service 696 (although the section east of Dartford to Horns Cross was replaced by buses).

Between 1935 and 1940 much of the LPTB tram network to the north of the river was converted primarily to trolleybus operation; had war not broken out again in September 1939, the surviving routes south of the river would have followed. As it was, the wartime years gave London's trams a stay of execution and it would be a decade before the process of final abandonment took place and by 1950, when the programme of replacement recommenced, it would be the motorbus – rather than the trolleybus – that was preferred.

The war years inevitably resulted in considerable damage to the infrastructure of the network, with sections of route requiring replacement and trams being destroyed. On 8 September 1940, for example, 29 trams were destroyed when a bomb hit Camberwell depot.

The post-war years

After the war the immediate priority was to see services restored rather than immediately seek tramcar replacement. There was, as a result, a considerable amount expended on maintenance – both infrastructure and vehicles – immediately post-war, but conversion remained the eventual policy.

The creation of the London Transport Executive, following the Transport Act 1947, on 1 January 1948 brought new masters but no change of heart as far as the future of the trams was concerned. On 5 July 1950, Lord Latham, the chairman of the LTE, announced that the surviving trams were to be replaced in a programme codenamed

'Operation Tramaway' over the next three years. The work was estimated to cost some £10 million and be completed in nine stages (in reality it was completed in two years in only eight stages).

'Operation Tramaway'

The first stages in the conversion programme affected primarily routes in south and south-west London. It was not until Stage 4, on 10/11 July 1951, that the programme affected the south-east. The routes affected were the 68 from Waterloo and the 70 from London Bridge that both operated via Rotherhithe to Greenwich.

The next stage – over the weekend of 6/7 October 1951 – saw the elimination of tram operation via Dog Kennel Hill with the conversion of the routes serving Peckham Rye, Forest Hill via Dulwich, Lewisham Clock Tower (via Rushey Green) and Blackwall Tunnel.

There were three stages in the programme in 1952. The first of these – over the weekend of 5/6 January – affected all the services to Grove Park – the 52, 54 and 74. The penultimate conversion – on 5/6 April 1952 – covered the surviving routes that made use of the Kingsway Subway; this included the 35 from Forest Hill and resulted in the final elimination of tram services on the section from Forest Hill via Crofton Park to New Cross Gate.

The final conversion was to take place over the weekend of 5/6 July 1952. For the previous week, most trams operated with posters advertising the last tram week. The services affected were those serving Greenwich, Woolwich, Eltham, Plumstead and Abbey Wood. As the final trams arrived from their last duties, they were to make one final journey – to the scrapyard at Penhall Road, where the vast majority were dismantled in a process that continued through until early 1953.

A note on the photographs

The majority of the illustrations in this book have been drawn from the collection of the Online Transport Archive, a UK-registered charity that was set up to accommodate collections put together by transport enthusiasts who wished to see their precious images secured for the long-term. Further information about the archive can be found at: www.onlinetransportarchive.org or email secretary@onlinetransportarchive.org

Trams from two operators are pictured in Market Place, Bexleyheath. On the left is Bexley UDC No 16; this was the last of four additional trams – Nos 13-16 – that the council acquired in 1904 to supplement the 12 originally supplied the previous year for the opening of the tramway. All were built by the Electric Railway & Tramway Carriage Works Co Ltd and were initially fitted with Brush Type A four-wheel trucks. On the right is Dartford No 2; this was one of the 12 cars delivered in 1906 for the system's opening. Whilst the Dartford car was to be destroyed in the 1917 fire, No 16 was to survive – as did the other 32 passenger trams in the Bexley fleet – to July 1933 and the creation of the LPTB. The ex-Bexley cars were allocated the new fleet numbers 2066-98 but, due to their poor condition, Nos 1-16 had been withdrawn by the middle of July 1933 without being renumbered.

As a schoolboy looks on, the photographer records three trams in Beresford Square, Woolwich. As a result of the transfer of a short distance of track in Plumstead to the LCC, which allowed for the construction of the route through to Abbey Wood, the LCC granted Bexley UDC the right to operate a through service to Woolwich. This scene, thus, records one of the ex-LCC 'B' class trams – Bexley No 22 – with two LCC 'E/1' class trams – including No 856. 'E/1' No 856 was one of the batch built in 1907 for the LCC by Hurst Nelson that were fitted with Mountain & Gibson bogies. It was scrapped in February 1939 as a result of the pre-war conversion programme.

DARTFORD COUNCIL LIGHT RAILWAYS

Recorded on a postcard franked on 19 August 1915, Dartford Council Light Railways No 8 is seen ascending West Hill as it makes its way from the town centre towards Gravel Hill and Bexleyheath. For the opening of the system United Electric Car Co Ltd supplied 12 open-top trams – Nos 1–12 – that were fitted with Brill 21E four-wheel trucks. All 12 were to be destroyed in the disastrous depot fire of August 1917. The Dartford system was very much an outpost of the eventual LPTB network.

Three of the 12-car fleet operated by Dartford Council Light Railways are posed inside the council's tram depot. The depot was situated on Victoria Road, a short distance beyond the terminus, and was built adjacent to the council's power station; the latter was used to supply the power used by the tramway. The depot and the council's entire tramcar fleet was destroyed by fire overnight on 6/7 August 1917. Monday 6 August had been a bank holiday and the trams had been particularly busy that day. Following investigation, the usual cause of depot fires – an electrical fault – was discounted and the blame was laid in all probability upon a carelessly thrown cigarette butt. The total damage was estimated to have cost £17,000 – or the equivalent of almost £1.2 million at 2020 prices – and the building was not rebuilt. Thereafter, tram services in Dartford were operated by trams based at Bexley's depot on Broadway.

DARTFORD HOSPITAL

The late 19th and early 20th centuries saw the construction of a number of hospitals designed to cater for diseases such as smallpox that required patients to be isolated. One such facility – the Joyce Green – was developed near Dartford and, as the site expanded, it was provided with a 4ft 0in gauge horse-operated tramway. This view, taken in the mid-1920s, records five trams in front of the depot. From 1925, the trams were hauled by petrol-powered ambulances. Use of the tramway ceased in the mid-1930s.

Bexley UDC hired and then purchased a number of ex-LCC 'B' class trams during World War I; these were partly to cater for increased traffic during the war and partly to provide services in Dartford following the disastrous fire of August 1917. The 'B' class, which dated originally to 1903, had originally been built as open-top by the Electric Railway & Tramway Carriage Works Co Ltd but those operated by the joint committee established in 1921 between Bexley and Dartford councils had already received fully-enclosed top covers. A total of 17 were eventually purchased out of the 23 operated; the other six were returned to the LCC. Here No 30, in the joint committee's brown and cream livery, is seen at the Horns Cross terminus in 1928. Although the original Bexley cars, Nos 1-16, were quickly disposed of after the LPTB takeover, the 'B' class – Nos 23-39 – were spruced up and received 'C' suffixes after their original fleet numbers pending renumbering; this was, however, never undertaken and all 17 were withdrawn by mid-October 1933. The Horns Cross service became route 96 under the LPTB. The 96 was an early conversion; the section from Woolwich to Dartford was taken over by trolleybuses on route 696 on Sunday, 24 November 1935. The section from Dartford to Horns Cross was not replaced by trolleybuses but by motorbuses on route 480 at the same time.

ERITH

For the opening of the Erith UDC network in 1905 Brush supplied 14 double-deck trams fitted with Mountain & Gibson 21EM four-wheel trucks. Half were open-top, with the other seven – including No 11, seen here – being equipped from new with open-balcony top covers. At the creation of the LPTB in July 1933, Erith UDC possessed 19 trams; these were allocated the fleet numbers 2099-117, although these numbers were never carried, with the fleet being initially renumbered with the suffix 'D' after their original Erith fleet numbers. The seven open-top cars were quickly withdrawn, as were the four ex-LUT cars – Nos 15-18 – and the ex-Kingston-upon-Hull No 19.

The seven open-balcony cars – Nos 7, 8, 10-14 – were, however, to have a longer life with the LPTB. Shortly after the new organisation came into being, these seven trams were re-equipped with Brill 21E four-wheel trucks reused from ex-Croydon Corporation trams. The seven were also repainted into LPTB red – as illustrated here by No 10D, carrying its new suffix – and modified to carry ex-LCC pattern route boards. Six of the seven were to survive in service until the local routes were converted to trolleybus operation on 9/10 November 1935 before being scrapped at Brixton Hill depot in February 1936; the exception was No 10D, which was scrapped in October 1935.

LONDON COUNTY COUNCIL

The LCC was the dominant tramway operator in south-east London and contributed the bulk of the network featured in this volume. This undated view records 'E/1' No 1244 – one of a batch delivered during 1908 and 1909 – heading inbound along New Kent Road with a service towards Blackfriars Bridge. Behind is 'C' class No 234; this was one of a batch of 100 trams, originally open-top, that were built by Brush and fitted with Brill 21E four-wheel trucks for the conversion of the routes to New Cross and Greenwich. All the 'C' class were withdrawn between 1924 and 1931, although a number were subsequently converted into snowploughs. Metropolitan Police regulations required that the lower-deck vestibules were kept open; it was not until the end of the LCC era that these regulations were relaxed to permit fully-enclosed trams.

SOUTHWARK BRIDGE

With evidence of wartime precautions and damage – most notably to Cannon Street station in the background (most of the glazing from the overall roof had been removed to safeguard it prior to the outbreak of war but the station had still been seriously damaged during the Blitz) – 'HR/2' No 1857 stands at the terminus at Southwark Bridge prior to heading outbound to Woolwich with a service on route 46. Southwark Bridge was the closest point to the City of London that trams from south London reached; trams had originally crossed the river to the north bank, but wartime damage to the bridge resulted in the terminus being slightly cut back. After the war, the terminus was used by routes 6 and 10 (towards Tooting), both of which were converted over the weekend of 6/7 January 1951, 48 to West Norwood and 52 to Grove Park, which both succumbed over the weekend of 5/6 January 1952, and 46, which was to be one of the last routes converted in July 1952.

BLACKFRIARS ROAD

Pictured turning right from Southwark Street into Blackfriars Road heading towards Blackfriars Bridge on 12 May 1950 is 'Rehab' 'E/1' No 1766 heading towards Clapham Junction with a service on route 26. Before World War II the 26 had operated beyond Clapham to run via Putney Bridge and Hammersmith to Kew Bridge. The section from the Borough terminus at the Hop Exchange, which was one of the two termini that served London Bridge, along Southwark Street was served post-war by two services; alongside the 26 was the 12, which ran via Battersea to Wandsworth High Street. The 12 and the 26 were casualties of the first stage of Operation Tramaway on 30 September/1 October 1950. At the same time, however, route 72 was extended from Savoy Street over Blackfriars Bridge to serve Southwark Street; this extension remained in

service until 10/11 July 1951 when, as part of Stage 4, the 72 was cut back to its original Savoy Street terminus and trams ceased to use the section along Southwark Street. No 1766 was also a casualty of Stage 1, being scrapped at Penhall Road in November 1950.

TOOLEY STREET

With the vast bulk of London Bridge station on the left overshadowing the scene, two of the 1931 batch of 'E/1s' – Nos 555 and 586 – are seen at the Tooley Street terminus of route 70 on 10 June 1951. Tooley Street was the second of the two termini to serve London Bridge and was approached by a short section of single track – visible in the foreground – before the double-track terminus. The only route to make use of the section of Tooley Street north of the junction with Tower Bridge Road was the 70, and so this section was last used by trams on 10 July 1951 as part of Stage 4 of 'Operation Tramaway'.

Having just turned left from Tooley Street, 'E/1' No 591 – one of the 1931 batch constructed reusing equipment from redundant 'F' and 'G' class single-deckers – is passing the crossover at the north end of Tower Bridge Road with the famous bridge in the background. The 68 – from Greenwich to Waterloo – was the only daily service to use the section from Tooley Street to Bricklayers Arms and thus tram operation along this stretch ceased on 10/11 July 1951, when routes 68 and 70 were converted.

BRICKLAYERS ARMS

Approaching the photographer from Tower Bridge Road at Bricklayers Arms with a service on route 68 towards Waterloo is another of the 1931 batch of 'E/1s' No 554. The tram will take New Kent Road towards Elephant & Castle. Great Dover Street, heading to the north-west at this point, was used by routes 46 and 52, whilst, apart from the 68, New Kent Road was used by services 36, 38 and 74 that all turned right at the junction to join the 46 and 52 in heading south-eastwards along Old Kent Road towards New Cross. In the 70 or so years since this photograph was taken, this location has become unrecognisable; the junction has been replaced by a giant roundabout with flyover and all the buildings – even the pub that gave the junction its name – have been swept away.

On 20 April 1951, 'HR/2' No 120 has just departed from Elephant & Castle with a service on route 56 towards Peckham Rye and is making use of the short single-track section that linked Newington Causeway with Walworth Road; the latter can be seen in the foreground. Nos 101-59 were built by Hurst Nelson during 1931 and were fitted with radial-arm bogies supplied by the Electro-Mechanical Brake Co Ltd. Eight of the batch – Nos 112/23-25/29-31/48 – were destroyed during the war. None were fitted with trolleypoles and so the type was rendered redundant when the last of the all-conduit routes – the 35 – was converted to bus operation in April 1952; by this date, only three of the type – Nos 118/20/21 – remained operational.

BERMONDSEY

Between Dock Head and Lower Road, Rotherhithe, there was a short section of single track with two passing loops along Jamaica Road and Union Road in Bermondsey and, on 10 June 1951, 'E/1' No 936 is recorded heading eastbound with a service towards Greenwich on route along the single-track section adjacent to Wilson Grove on Jamaica Road. This section of track was used by two routes to Greenwich church – the 68 from Waterloo and the 70 from London Bridge – and these services were converted to bus operation as part of Stage 4 of 'Operation Tramaway' on 10/11 July 1951. Theoretically, Stage 4 should have encompassed the conversion of the surviving routes through the Kingsway Subway, but delays in the construction of the new Stockwell bus garage meant that the conversion of routes 68 and 70 was brought forward. Stage 4 was the smallest stage in the conversion programme and was also unusual in being the only stage undertaken mid-week; the last trams operated on the Tuesday, with the replacement buses taking over on the following day.

Routes 68 and 70 operated through Bermondsey, Rotherhithe and Deptford; there was a bridge at Deptford across the creek and, in 1949, it became necessary to provide a temporary new bridge – complete with conduit track – to replace the existing structure. On 10 July 1949 'E/1' No 553 was the first passenger car to make use of the new – temporary – inbound track; it was not until later in the month that the replacement outbound track was brought into service. Although there were plans to include the trams in the new bridge at this site, the decision to advance the conversion of routes 68 and 70 in lieu of the Kingsway Subway services meant that the services continued to use the temporary bridge until they were converted to bus operation in July 1951. No 553 was one of the final 50 'E/1' class trams to be constructed – in 1931 – that reused equipment from the 'F' and 'G' class single-deck trams that had been rendered redundant as a result of the decision to modernise the Kingsway Subway to accommodate double-deck trams.

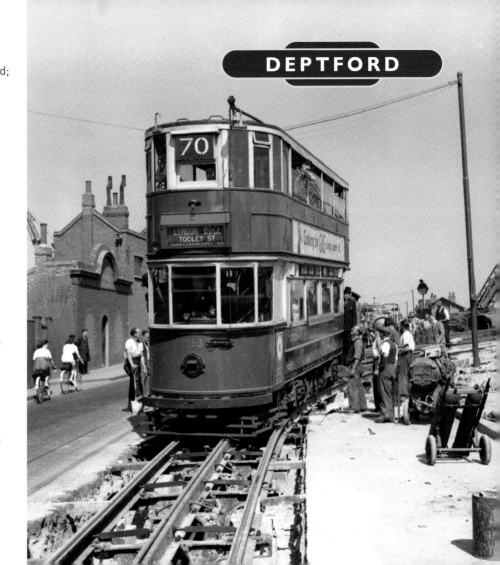

DEPTFORD

Seen passing Greenwich town hall on 12 August 1951 is 'HR/2' No 120 with a service on route 58 towards Victoria. The tram will turn left at this point to take South Street towards Lewisham. The track in the foreground along Greenwich High Road was used by services 36, 38 and 40 and so remained operational until the final abandonment on 5 July 1952. The Grade II listed town hall was designed by Clifford Culpin and built by William Moss & Sons. Completed in 1939, it was modified internally by the Rolfe Judd Practice between 1972 and 1974 and is now known as the Borough Hall and Meridian House, with Woolwich town hall being used as headquarters of the London Borough of Greenwich. The redundant Greenwich building is now occupied by the Greenwich School of Management (GSM London) and Greenwich Dance.

On the same day, another 'HR/2' – No 105 – is pictured emerging from Blackwall Lane into Trafalgar Road with an inbound service towards Victoria via Lewisham, Catford and Dog Kennel Hill. The track heading off to the right was used by services between Greenwich and Woolwich, including the 36, 38 and 40 that were amongst the services to survive until the final conversion in July 1952.

BLACKWALL TUNNEL

With the southern entrance of Blackwall Tunnel in the background, 'HR/2' No 134 is seen awaiting departure with a service on route 58 towards Victoria via Dog Kennel Hill. This was the only service to Blackwall Tunnel and was to be converted to bus operation over the weekend of 6/7 October 1951 as part of Stage 5 of 'Operation Tramaway'. No 134 was part of the batch of 'HR/2s' that were not equipped with trolleypoles and thus limited to operation of the conduit routes only. With the demise of the routes such as the 58 that operated via Dog Kennel Hill, the majority of the type – with the exception of 12 that were transferred to New Cross depot for use on route 35 – were taken out of service following the October 1951 conversions.

No 134 was scrapped at Penhall Road – known as the 'Tramatorium' – in March 1952. The original Blackwall Tunnel was designed by Sir Alexander Binnie and constructed between 1892 and 1897; it was officially opened by the Prince of Wales – the future King Edward VII – on 22 May 1897. The impressive building over the tunnel entrance – known as Southern Tunnel House – was designed by Thomas Blashil, the LCC's architect; this is still extant and is now listed Grade II. The second tunnel, long planned to cope with additional traffic, was officially opened on 2 August 1967.

WOOLWICH

With the Fortune of War public house, which was demolished in the early 1980s, situated on Woolwich New Road in the background, ex-Leyton 'E/3' No 176 has just departed from Beresford Square – the terminus of routes 44, 46 and 72 – with a service on route 46 via Eltham church towards New Cross Gate. The date is towards the end of June 1952, as No 176 carries the posters noting the last tram week in place of adverts. No 176 was one of 50 trams acquired by the LCC on behalf of Leyton UDC from English Electric in 1931. Although the Leyton system remained owned by the UDC until the creation of the LPTB, it was operated by the LCC from 1921 and the 50 trams – Nos 161-210 – were similar to the LCC's 'E/3' class, albeit fitted with enclosed lower-deck vestibules from new. Following the conversion of the tram routes in east London, the batch was transferred south of the river and 16 remained in service until the final abandonment on 5 July 1952.

On 22 April 1951, 'E/1' class No 1836 – one of the type that was modified with external lower-deck side-strengthening bars after World War II – is seen in Beresford Square having just arrived with a service from the City of London on route 46 as two trolleybuses pass in the background. Beresford Square was, by this time, the terminus for three routes that ran southwards via Shooters Hill. The 44 and the 46 ran via Eltham Church with the former terminating at Middle Park Avenue whilst the latter ran via New Cross Gate and Bricklayers Arms to the south side of Southwark Bridge. The third service that terminated – the 72 – ran direct to Eltham then via New Cross Gate and the Elephant & Castle to terminate at Savoy Street on the Embankment. These routes were amongst the last to survive, being converted over the final weekend of London tram operation on 5/6 July 1952.

PLUMSTEAD

Between Plumstead Road and McLeod Road on the route towards Abbey Wood there was a section of single track with passing loops along Plumstead High Street. Surviving until the final conversion of the system in July 1952, Plumstead High Street was destined to become the last significant two-way single-track section on the London system. Pictured emerging from Plumstead Road into Beresford Square with a service on route 38 is No 94. This was one of 20 trams – Nos 81-100 – that were similar to the LCC's 'E/1' class and built by Brush during 1927 and 1928 for East Ham Corporation. Five of the batch received lower-deck windscreens before World War II and were transferred to Abbey Wood; the remaining 15 – including No 94 – were stored in Hampstead depot following the conversion of the last east London routes. During the war, the stored trams were gradually fitted with lower-deck windscreens and restored to service to replace trams destroyed by enemy action. With the exception of No 81 – withdrawn earlier in 1952 – all of the batch survived in service until July 1952.

Pictured in April 1952 at the Abbey Wood terminus of routes 36 and 38 – the former operated anticlockwise along the Embankment and the latter clockwise – are 'E/3' No 2000 and ex-West Ham No 311. The track running towards the photographer was the connection to Abbey Wood depot. The services to Abbey Wood were amongst those that survived to be converted to bus operation during the final stage of 'Operation Tramaway' over the weekend of 5/6 July 1952. No 311 was one of a batch of 17 trams delivered to West Ham Corporation – as Nos 69-85 – during 1929 and 1930. Renumbered 296-312 by the LPTB, the trams, which had been built by Hurst Nelson, were fitted with lower-deck windscreens and, following the conversion of the final routes in east London, were transferred to Abbey Wood and New Cross depots. A number were to survive in service right through until the final conversions and the last of the batch were not scrapped until November 1952.

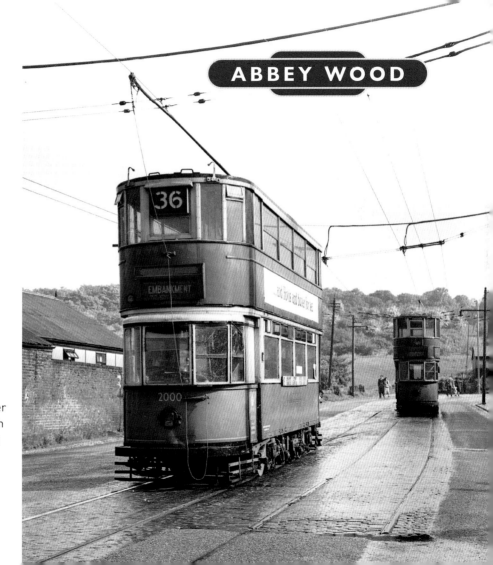

HORNS CROSS

The terminus of the erstwhile Dartford system at Horns Cross was the easternmost extremity of the tramways operated by the LPTB south of the river and it at this terminus that 'M' class No 1696 is pictured. Following the creation of the LPTB, the trams operated by the Bexley and Dartford joint committee were swiftly replaced by ex-LCC 'M' class trams that had been in store. The 'M' class represented a four-wheel version of the 'E/1' and had been built in 1910; the first car – No 1427 – had been built by the LCC, with Nos 1428-76 by Hurst Nelson and Nos 1677-1726 by Brush. All were fitted with four-wheel trucks supplied by Heenan & Froude; the unusual design, clearly visible in this side view, included pressed steel sideframes and swing bolsters. The tram service to Horns Cross was allocated the route number 96. Tram operation of the service by the LPTB was not to survive long; the section between Woolwich and Dartford was converted to trolleybus service 696 on 24 November 1935, with the route beyond Dartford being converted to motorbus as Country Area route 480.

BEXLEYHEATH

The penultimate numerically of the Brush-built 'M' class trams – No 1725 – is pictured in Bexleyheath heading eastbound with a service towards Dartford on route 96. The conversion of the routes north of the river alongside those east of Woolwich to trolleybus operation rendered the 'M' class surplus to requirements and all 97 survivors – Nos 1441, 1444 and 1446 had been rebuilt by the LCC as Class ME/3 in 1933 prior to the creation of the LPTB – were scrapped between September 1934 and March 1938 with No 1725 – note the LCC-style fleet number despite having been repainted into London Transport livery – succumbing in July 1937. This view also shows to good effect the impact of the 1870 Tramways Act in terms of the road layout; the central cobbled section – extending 18 inches outside the running track – was maintained by the tramway operator, with the remainder the responsibility of the highway authority.

ACADEMY ROAD

On 17 June 1952, one of the 'Tunnel Rebuild' 'E/1s' – No 565 makes its way along Academy Road with a service on route 46 from Woolwich towards Southwark. The tram will continue inbound via Eltham Church and Lewisham. The final 50 of the 'E/1' class – Nos 552-601 – were all completed during 1930 and made use of bogies reused from the single-deck trams rendered redundant by the rebuilding of the Kingsway Subway fitted to new double-deck bodies supplied by English Electric at a price of £2,000 each. Originally built with open lower-deck vestibules, all received windscreens during 1939. Two – Nos 583 and 597 – were wartime losses with the remainder being withdrawn between late 1949 and the final conversion of the system.

ELTHAM HILL

In April 1952, 'E/3' No 1945 approaches the Yorkshire Grey roundabout from Eltham Hill with a service on route 46 from Woolwich, via Eltham Church, New Cross and Old Kent Road, to Southwark Bridge. The roundabout at the junction of Eltham Hill, Eltham Road and Westhorne Avenue was served by three routes: the 46 that used Eltham Road and Eltham Hill, the 72 that used Westhorne Avenue to bypass Eltham itself and the 44 that terminated at the roundabout. The section along Westhorne Road opened on 30 June 1932 and represented the last extension opened by the LCC, with the modified layout involving the roundabout being opened on 25 August 1935; there were plans to extend further – to provide a connection with Grove Park – but the replacement of the LCC by the LPTB meant that these plans were not progressed.

ELTHAM CHURCH

During 1927 and 1928, East Ham Corporation took delivery of 20 trams that were virtually identical to the LCC 'E/1' class; these became LPTB Nos 81-100. Five were transferred south of the river in 1939, with the remainder stored. The remaining 15 were reinstated to replace wartime losses and, on 18 June 1952, No 93 is pictured turning the corner from Well Hall Road into Eltham Hill in Eltham with a service on route 44 from Woolwich. This route, which did not penetrate the central area, was trolley-operated throughout. All of the batch bar No 81, which was withdrawn in April 1952, survived until the final conversion of the system in July 1952.

Pictured alongside the clock tower at Lewisham, as a policeman gives directions, on 26 August 1951 is 'HR/2' class No 116 heading towards Blackwall Tunnel with a service on route 58. The clock tower was the terminus for route 62 on Saturdays, which operated from Camberwell via Dog Kennel Hill and Forest Hill to reach Lewisham. The section the 58 will take towards Greenwich via Lewisham Road and South Street was the final significant stretch of single track with passing loops operated by London trams apart a section of the Abbey Wood route in Plumstead. Lewisham to Greenwich was one of the sections from which all tram services were withdrawn in early October 1951 when the routes via Dog Kennel Hill were converted to bus operation. The line heading off to the left of the clock tower headed towards New Cross Gate and was used at this date by the 46 and 72 towards Southwark Bridge and Savoy Street respectively. The clock tower, constructed in Portland stone, was completed in 1900 to mark Queen Victoria's Diamond Jubilee of 1897.

On 10 July 1949, Class E/1 No 1007 is pictured turning from Catford Road into Bromley Road with a service on route 74 towards Grove Park. There was a triangular junction at this point. At the time that the photographer recorded the view the track from Catford Road turning northwards into Rushey Green was used by trams on routes 58 and 62 heading to Blackwall Tunnel and Lewisham clock tower respectively; these services were converted as part of Stage 5 of 'Operation Tramaway' in October 1951. The 74 was the only route to use the west-to-south curve whilst trams on routes 52 and 54 from Grove Park headed due north to run alongside routes 58 and 62 to Lewisham before heading inbound via New Cross Gate to the City and Victoria respectively. The last trams passed through Catford in early January 1952 with the conversion of routes 52, 54 and 74.

GROVE PARK

On 27 August 1949, two rehabilitated Class E/1s, Nos 1310 and 1491, are pictured at the Grove Park terminus of route 54. This service, which ran through to Victoria via Lewisham Camberwell Green and Vauxhall, was one of three that terminated post-war at Grove Park and was one of the busiest tram routes to operate in London after 1945; the other two were the 52 that ran via Lewisham and Bricklayers Arms to the south end of Southwark Bridge and the 74, which operated via Crofton Park, Brockley, Bricklayers Arms and Elephant & Castle to Blackfriars. All three routes were converted to bus operation over the weekend of 5/6 January 1952.

Heading north along Brockley Road towards New Cross, the trams operated a one-way system, running northbound via Shardeloes Road and southbound via Malpas Road. Seen here on 29 September 1951, three trams are seen heading northbound; in the distance there are two 'E/1s', No 1841 and 1414, en route from Grove Park towards Blackfriars station whilst in the foreground, No 392 is about to pass to pass the Brockley Cross crossover with a service on route 66 from Forest Hill to Victoria. The 66, which was regularly allocated to the older cars in the fleet, was one of the routes converted to bus operation as part of Stage 5 of 'Operation Tramaway' in October 1951. This left the section through Brockley Cross operated by only route 74; this was to persist until the next stage of the conversion programme – in early January 1952

– when route 74 was converted. No 392 was one of 25 trams similar to the LCC's 'E/1' class that were purchased by Croydon Corporation during 1927 and 1928; originally numbered 31-55, the trams were built by Hurst Nelson and became Nos 375-99 in July 1933. Four of the batch – Nos 376/79/80/98 – were amongst the trams that underwent the rehabilitation programme in the late 1930s and one – No 396 – was destroyed during World War II. Another – No 376 – was destroyed by fire in 1945; the remainder, following the conversion of the Croydon routes, were transferred to New Cross depot, where they survived until withdrawal between October 1951 and January 1952.

Heading south from New Cross Gate on a route 35 service towards Forest Hill along the single-track section along Malpas Road is 'E/3' No 1932 in March 1952. The 35 was the last tram route to serve Forest Hill. Prior to Stage 5 of 'Operation Tramaway' in October 1951, the main road – London Road and Waldram Park Road – had been served by routes 58 and 62 that approached from the west, having descended Dog Kennel Hill en route to Blackwall Tunnel and Lewisham Clock Tower respectively as well as the 66, which terminated at Forest Hill, from Victoria. This service operated in parallel with the 35 from Camberwell. The 'E/3' class represented 100 trams – Nos 1904-2003 – acquired by the LCC during 1931; they were built by Hurst Nelson and fitted with bogies supplied by the Electro-Mechanical Brake Co Ltd. They were delivered for operation through the Kingsway Subway following its rebuilding to permit double-deck tram operation. Eight of the batch were destroyed by enemy action during World War II; the remainder were all withdrawn and scrapped from late 1951 onwards.

FOREST HILL

On Saturday 6 October, 1951 'HR/2' No 153 waits to access the stub terminus on Perry Vale, Forest Hill, that is currently occupied by 'E/1' 1660, about to depart on route 66 to Victoria. Note, in the foreground, the point lever that operated the point at the junction of Waldram Park Road and Perry Vale; this was to be the last day on which the lever would be required, as services on Waldram Crescent westwards – the 58, 60 and 62 – were all to be last operated by tram that Saturday. The 66 was also converted to bus operation over the same weekend, leaving Forest Hill to be served solely by the 35 until the conversion of the surviving Kingsway subway routes in April 1952.

GOOSE GREEN

On 29 July 1949, 'HR/2' No 1859 is seen at the Goose Green crossover, on Lordship lane, with an outbound service towards Forest Hill on route 62. Nos 1854-903 were the first of the 'HR/2s' to be constructed, being built by English Electric in 1930. They were equipped with equal-wheel bogies supplied by the Electro-Mechanical Brake Co Ltd and, unlike the later batch, also incorporated double trolleypoles. Of the 50, four – Nos 1884/85/87/90 – underwent the rehabilitation programme whilst three – Nos 1881/83/86 – were sold pre-war to Leeds Corporation and eight – Nos 1865/89/98-903 – were destroyed during the war. The remainder were all withdrawn between 1950 and 1952, with one – No 1858 – being secured for preservation; this is now operational at the East Anglia Transport Museum.

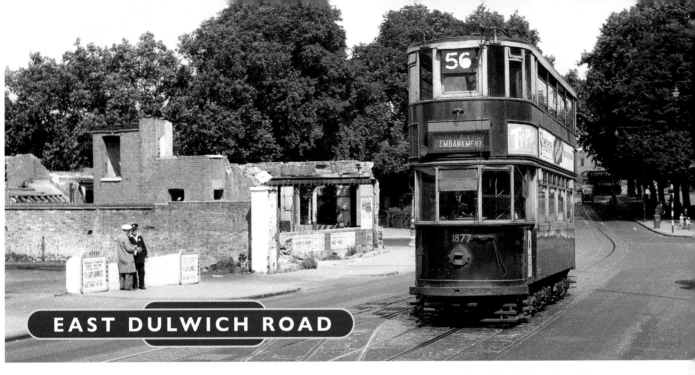

EAST DULWICH ROAD

Class 'HR/2' No 1877 has just departed from the Peckham Rye terminus on 29 July 1949 as it is seen passing one of the two crossovers on East Dulwich Road as it descends past Goose Green on its way to the junction with Lordship Lane. The tram will then head westwards to ascend Dog Kennel Hill en route to the Embankment on route 56. Post-war, Peckham Rye was served by two routes – the 56 and the 84 – that ran in parallel to Elephant & Castle, where they divided. The 56 then proceeded clockwise via Westminster and the Embankment and back to Elephant & Castle via Blackfriars, whilst the 84 made the trip in an anticlockwise direction, heading initially to Blackfriars from Elephant & Castle. The services to Peckham Rye were converted to bus operation over the weekend of 6/7 October 1951 as part of Stage 5 of 'Operation Tramaway'.

DOG KENNEL HILL

On 22 September 1951, 'HR/2' No 1868 is pictured en route to Dulwich Library with a service on route 60 having just descended the four-track section on Dog Kennel Hill. The 60 was a weekday peak-hour-only service from Southwark Bridge. When the section up Dog Kennel Hill had first opened in 1906, the Board of Trade had insisted that only one tram should be on any track at a time in order to avoid the possibility of a collision caused by a runaway tram. This severely restricted capacity and so resulted in the section being quadrupled. Cars heading down the hill were faced by two compulsory stops – one at the top and one midway down the descent – with trams heading uphill non-stop. Since the demise of the trams, the road has been converted into a dual carriageway, with the central reservation running effectively in the space occupied by the innermost pair of running lines.

Pictured turning right on 9 September 1951 from Camberwell New Road in Denmark Hill with a service towards Blackwall Tunnel on route 58 is 'HR/2' No 105. Four services post-war operated along Camberwell New Road; one service – the 58 – headed along Denmark Hill from this point whilst the other three – the 40, 58 and 72 – headed straight on along Church Street towards New Cross. A significant number of routes made use of Walworth Road towards Camberwell Green; the 35 and 66 joined the 40 and 72 heading towards New Cross whilst the 34, 48, 56, 60, 62 and 84 all headed into Denmark Hill. Of these, the 56, 60, 62 and 84 joined the 58 in heading towards Dog Kennel Hill with the 34 and 48 turning right quickly into Coldharbour Lane. The Dog Kennel Hill services were all converted as part of Stage 5 of 'Operation Tramaway' on 6/7 October 1951.

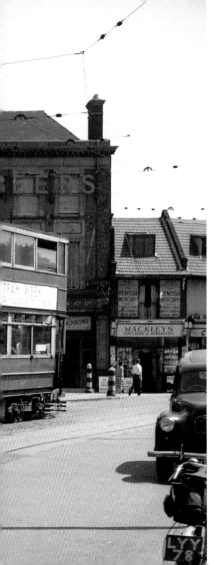

THE LAST DAY

It's 5 July 1952 and almost a century of tramcar operation in London is about to come to an end. Two trams – a Class E/3 and 'Subway Rebuild' E/1 No 592 – are seen at Beresford Square awaiting departure with services on route 46 towards Southwark Bridge. The two display the 'Last Tram Week' posters that were a feature of the trams during the week leading up to the fateful Saturday whilst the tram closest to the photographer bears some of the chalk graffiti that was a feature of many of the trams that operated on this last day. No 87 was to achieve fame as the final obsequies for the trams took place as it was the last tram to make use of the Woolwich change pit as it made its final journey. The much-delayed No 87 had been running very late on its last trip from New Cross. The plough shifter at Beresford Square had been asked to wait for No 592 to come through from Abbey Wood depot. He then went home not aware that No 87 was still on the tracks. No 87 was, therefore, the last tram to use the Beresford Square plough shift. The crew did the work, with Ken Thorpe, a Charlton Works employee, witnessing this. Enthusiasts on board were permitted to travel on No 87 to Penhall Road. The last trams arrived at New Cross depot at 1.15am on the Sunday morning to be greeted by a crowd and by the chairman of the London Transport Executive, Lord Latham, who spoke the immortal lines 'Goodbye, old tram' as the onlookers bade farewell to the tram for the last time. The last tram to operate in service was, in fact, No 87 that arrived at Beresford Square about 2.30am whilst the last movement saw No 1931 travel from New Cross to Penhall Road at about 3.30am.

PENHALL ROAD

In order to scrap the significant number of trams that would be made redundant as a result of the conversion programme, a storage site at Penhall Road – slightly to the east of Charlton works on Woolwich Road – was developed and, in July 1950, Class E/1 No 1322 had the dubious distinction of being disposed at the yard in a test in order to gauge the local reaction to the work. The site became known as the 'Tramatorium' as almost 800 trams were eventually disposed of between then and January 1953. Seen awaiting their fate in November 1951 are four 'HR/2s' – Nos 113/20/27/37 – and two unidentified trams; although relatively new – dating from 1931 – this batch of trams was withdrawn relatively early as, lacking trolleypoles, they could not operate on the overhead sections of the routes destined to be operational into the final stages. Less than a decade after the last trams were scrapped, the 'Tramatorium' was to see the demise of another type of electric transport, as some of London's trolleybuses were broken up here between March and September 1959.

CREDITS

Lost Tramways of England – London South-East. Published in Great Britain in 2021 by Graffeg Limited.

Written by Peter Waller copyright © 2021. Designed and produced by Graffeg Limited copyright © 2021.

Graffeg Limited, 24 Stradey Park Business Centre, Mwrwg Road, Llangennech, Llanelli, Carmarthenshire, SA14 8YP, Wales, UK. Tel: 01554 824000. www.graffeg.com.

ISBN 9781914079825

1 2 3 4 5 6 7 8 9

MIX
Paper from responsible sources
FSC® C014138
www.fsc.org

Photo credits

© Barry Cross Collection/Online Transport Archive: pages 14, 16, 17, 18, 21, 22, 23, 42.

© River Hospitals (Dartford)/Barry Cross Collection/Online Transport Archive: page 19.

© G. Robbins/Barry Cross Collection/Online Transport Archive: page 25.

© Phil Tatt/Online Transport Archive: pages 26, 38, 41, 45, 54, 63.

© John Meredith/Online Transport Archive: pages 27, 28, 29, 31, 32, 33, 49, 51, 52, 55, 56, 57, 58.

© Julian Thompson/Online Transport Archive: pages 30, 34, 35, 36, 39, 40, 44, 47, 48, 59.

© C. Carter: page 43.

© Neil Davenport/Online Transport Archive: page 60.

The photographs used in this book have come from a variety of sources. Wherever possible contributors have been identified although some images may have been used without credit or acknowledgement and if this is the case apologies are offered and full credit will be given in any future edition.

Cover: Beresford Square, Woolwich.
Back cover: Southwark Bridge, Victoria Road Depot, Erith.